IS IT LIVING OR NONLIVING?

by Lisa M. Bolt Simons

PEBBLE
a capstone imprint

Pebble Explore is published by Pebble, an imprint of Capstone.
1710 Roe Crest Drive
North Mankato, Minnesota 56003
www.capstonepub.com

Library of Congress Cataloging-in-Publication Data
Names: Bolt Simons, Lisa M., 1969- author.
Title: Is it living or nonliving? / Lisa M. Bolt Simons.
Description: North Mankato, Minnesota : Pebble, [2022] | Series: Science inquiry | Includes bibliographical references and index. | Audience: Ages 5-8 | Audience: Grades 2-3 | Summary: "Animals are living things. Rocks are nonliving. Why? Let's investigate the differences between living and nonliving things!"— Provided by publisher.
Identifiers: LCCN 2021002865 (print) | LCCN 2021002866 (ebook) | ISBN 9781977131416 (hardcover) | ISBN 9781977132581 (paperback) | ISBN 9781977154491 (pdf) | ISBN 9781977156167 (kindle edition)
Subjects: LCSH: Life (Biology)—Miscellanea—Juvenile literature. | Organisms—Miscellanea—Juvenile literature.
Classification: LCC QH309.2 .B65 2022 (print) | LCC QH309.2 (ebook) | DDC 570—dc23
LC record available at https://lccn.loc.gov/2021002865
LC ebook record available at https://lccn.loc.gov/2021002866

Image Credits
Getty Images/Samantha Mitchell/Corbis/VCG, 28; iStockphoto: FatCamera, 7, lmforthand, 29, MarcoAMazza, 19, ssj414, 5; Science Source/STEVE GSCHMEISSNER, 15; Shutterstock: Alex Tihonovs, 23, Arteck555, 11, Choksawatdikorn, 17, eva_blanco, 4, hans engbers, 1, 9, Ingus Kruklitis, 25, Iryna Kalamurza, 12, Jill Lang, 8, JRJfin, 21, Kenneth Sponsier, 22, Nuk2013, cover, Nurlan Mammadzada, 24, schankz, 27 (bottom), thka, 13, Vitaly Korovin, 27 (top), Zebra-Studio, 20

Artistic elements: Shutterstock/balabolka

Editorial Credits
Editor: Erika L. Shores; Designers: Dina Her and Juliette Peters; Media Researcher: Kelly Garvin; Production Specialist: Tori Abraham

All internet sites appearing in back matter were available and accurate when this book was sent to press.

TABLE OF CONTENTS

Words in **bold** are in the glossary.

INVESTIGATION: IS IT LIVING OR NONLIVING?

Your family just got a new puppy! How do you take care of it? You feed it. You give it water. Food and water will help the puppy grow. It may someday have its own puppies! A puppy is a living thing.

What if you have a pet rock? Will it eat food and drink water? Will it grow? Will it have baby rocks? If you said no, you're right! Rocks are not living things.

Now let's do an **investigation**.
Grab a piece of paper and a pencil.
Draw a line down the middle of the
paper. On one side write, "living."
On the other side write, "nonliving."

Go outside. Make **observations**.
Think about the puppy and the rock.
What needs water? What grows?
Draw pictures of three things you
think are living. Then label them. Draw
pictures of three things you think are
nonliving. Then label them.

HOW DO WE KNOW WHAT IS LIVING?

At first you may think that what moves is a living thing. A puppy moves! It's a living thing! Water moves. But it is not a living thing. A car moves. But it is not a living thing.

There are also living things that don't move. Think about mushrooms in a forest. Or think about coral deep in the sea. Living things have other **traits** besides movement. Let's learn about them!

Remember the puppy? The puppy is made of **cells**. Cells are the smallest parts of a living thing. You have cells too!

People have to give the puppy food and water. Scientists call food and water **nutrients**. These nutrients give the puppy energy. Nutrients also help the puppy grow. Being able to grow is a trait of a living thing. Nonliving things do not grow. The pet rock will never grow.

What are other traits of living things? If the puppy gets scared, it might run away. Or it might bark. It might even bite! The puppy is responding to its environment, or the world around it. Living things react to what is happening around them. The rock will never respond to anything around it. It will never be scared!

Finally, living things reproduce.
To reproduce means to make more
of their same kind.

WHICH THINGS ARE LIVING?

You can't see the smallest living things with your eyes. You need to look through a microscope! **Bacteria** are living things. A spoonful of lake water can have as many as 1 million bacteria cells. That's how small bacteria are! Each is made from a single cell. It moves. It eats. It also reproduces.

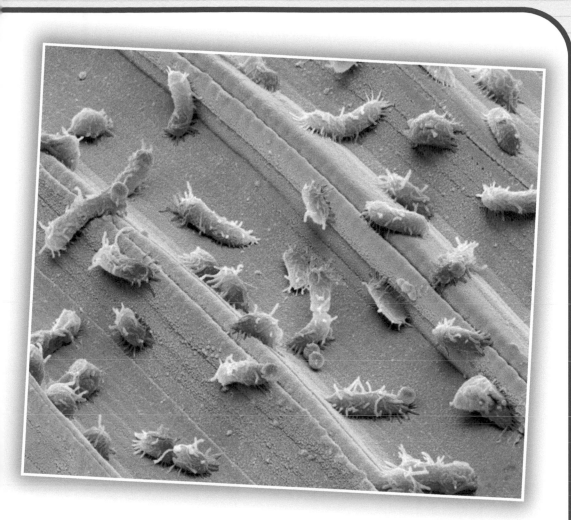

Some bacteria are good. They can help prepare food like cheese. Bacteria are also needed when making some medicines. Some bacteria are bad. They can cause sickness like strep throat.

Protozoans are also living things. They have single cells like bacteria. But they are bigger. Sometimes you can see protozoans without a microscope. There are more than 50,000 **species** of protozoans! These living things have a life cycle. They eat. They reproduce.

Protozoans are found in every habitat. Some species are not harmful to animals. But some can be dangerous. They can cause animals, including humans, to get very sick.

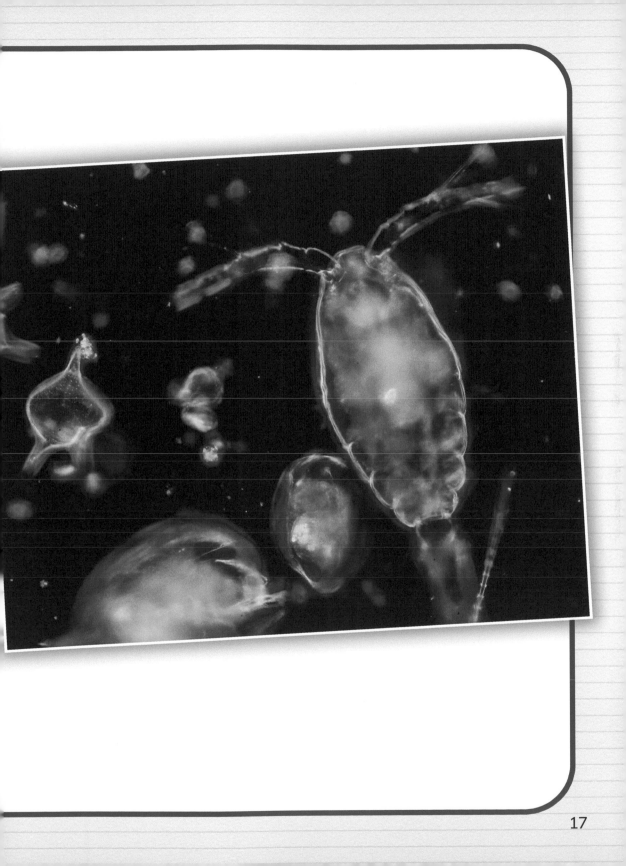

Have you ever seen the ocean? Did you see something that looks like long green grass in the water? If so, it might have been giant kelp. It can grow up to 164 feet (50 meters) long!

Giant kelp is a type of **chromist**. Chromists are living things. They grow. Most chromists use the sun to help make food. They reproduce. Other chromists can't be seen without a microscope.

Do you like mushrooms on pizza?
If so, you eat **fungi**! Fungi is a living
thing. Fungi has many cells. It grows.
It eats. It reproduces.

Fungi is found on land. It's also found
in water and in the air. Fungi is even
found in animals and plants!

Some fungi is used to help make medicine. Other fungi called mold is not good. That's what you find growing on old cheese or old leftover food. Yuck!

Remember your walk outside? Did you see any plants? Plants are living things, of course! They have many cells. They grow. They use the sun to help make food. They reproduce.

There are almost 400,000 species of plants. Most of these grow flowers. Plants make **oxygen** for living things to breathe. People and animals eat plants. Plants can help make medicines.

Pigeons are common birds in big cities.

What else did you see outside? What could be the last group of living things? That's right! Animals! Humans are a type of animal. Animals have many cells. They grow. They eat and drink. They reproduce.

Remember the puppy? Animals respond to their environment. They can find a warm, sunny spot if they get cold. They can run away if a bigger animal comes too close.

A turtle sits in the sun to warm up its body.

What happens when a living thing dies? Scientists say it is a living thing that is dead. The living thing used to be alive.

A nonliving thing was never alive, such as a pencil, a notebook, or an eraser. This also means nonliving things don't die.

Ask these questions to find out if something is living or nonliving:

- Does it have cells?
- Does it need food and water?
- Does it grow?
- Does it respond to its environment?
- Does it reproduce?

HOW DO WE TAKE CARE OF LIVING AND NONLIVING THINGS?

People take care of things differently. If a thing is living, it needs nutrients to grow. It's like the puppy. If it's nonliving, it doesn't need food or water. It's like the rock.

We don't give shoes nutrients. But we still take care of them. We keep shoes clean. We don't give a phone nutrients. But we still take care of it. We try not to drop a phone.

The world is full of living and nonliving things. What are all the living and nonliving things you take care of in your own life?

GLOSSARY

bacteria (bak-TEER-ee-uh)—one celled, tiny living things; some are helpful and some cause disease

cell (SEL)—a tiny structure that makes up all living things

chromist (KRO-mist)—a living thing that includes some algae and protozoans

fungi (FUHN-jy)—living things similar to a plant, but without flowers, leaves, or green coloring

investigation (in-vess-tuh-GAY-shuhn)—the search for facts to solve a problem or answer a question

nutrient (NOO-tree-uhnt)—a part of food that is used for growth

observation (ob-zur-VEY-shuhn)—to make note about what is seen or noticed

oxygen (OK-suh-juhn)—a colorless gas that people and animals breathe in order to live

protozoan (pro-toe-ZO-an)—a tiny living thing whose body is a single cell

species (SPEE-sheez)—a group of plants or animals that share common characteristics

trait (TRAYT)—a characteristic or feature

READ MORE

Davies, Nicola. *Many: The Diversity of Life on Earth.* Somerville, MA: Candlewick Press, 2017.

Kurtz, Kevin. *Living Things and Nonliving Things: A Compare and Contrast Book.* Mount Pleasant, SC: Arbordale Publishing, 2017.

Lukidis, Lydia. *A Real Live Pet!: Living vs. Nonliving.* New York: Kane Press, 2018.

INTERNET SITES

Fungi
ducksters.com/science/biology/fungi.php

Living and Non-Living Things
saburchill.com/chapters/chap0001.html

Living vs Non-Living Things
generationgenius.com/videolessons/living-vs-non-living-things-video-for-kids/

INDEX